My Dad at My Age

List of Rules

www.burfordparker.com

© 2018 Burford Parker

Other books coming soon from this author include

My Mum at My Age Santa at My Age
The Queen at My Age The President at My Age

My Dad at My Age
List of Rules

www.burfordparker.com
© 2018 Burford Parker

Published by
Node Central

The right of Burford Parker to be identified as the author of this work has been asserted in accordance with the Copyright, Designs and Patents Act 1988. All rights reserved. No portion of this book may be reproduced, stored in a retrieval system, or transmitted in any form without prior written permission from the author.

Illustrations by
Pavel Goldaev

For permissions contact
help@burfordparker.com

ISBN: 978-1-9160086-0-1

Emma & Ben,
Thanks for being the inspiration for this book.

My Dad at My Age
List of Rules

Burford Parker

I'm at an age where life should be fun,
not a care in the world, as long as I help my mum.

My dad on the other hand always sets the tone,
dishing out orders, while checking his phone.

Watching his head bounce from one screen to another,
he works so hard, will he ever recover?

If I go into his office, when he's at home for the day, he'll give me a strange look and tell me to go away.

My dad runs our house with military precision,
there's not much I can do, unless I ask for permission.

He repeatedly tells me what I can and can't do,
I'm surprised I'm allowed to tie up my shoe.

He's recently pinned a list of rules to my door,
there's so many on there, I can't keep track anymore.

High on that list is to be respectful and honest,
which is funny coming from him, as he often breaks his promise.

"I'll be finished in a minute", he'll say as I wait by his door, but that minute soon passes, then he adds many more.

I love playing games, but my dad's always the boss,
warning me of the dangers I might come across.

His stories about safety are getting harder to take,
I've heard them so often, they give me a headache!

Surrounded by screens, he doesn't know what I've found,
for I've got a magic crystal that can turn things around.

On the days he works late, I hardly see him at all,
but that will soon change when I make him small.

The power of this gem is a sight to behold,
it can reverse someone's life, so they never got old.

I can change my dad into any age I choose,
making everyday playtime, which is hard to refuse.

With a wave of my crystal, the lights flicker and then dim,
my dad's magically transformed into a younger version of him.

He's been reduced in size to something I can reach,
his face is much rounder, like a juicy giant peach.

It's still my dad, but not as I know him to be,
his eyes have more sparkle and he's grinning at me.

It's amazing how much we look like each other,
if anyone could see us, they'd think he was my brother.

The stress he's been under has disappeared without a trace, replaced by a desire to get out of his workplace.

We run down the corridor without a care anymore, only for Dad to get distracted by the rules on my door.

The list just goes on, like it's never going to end,
some of his restrictions are hard to comprehend.

I'm not sure he realises how many he's written,
there's more than a school, but less than a prison.

First on the list is to stop
having so much fun.
If I had my way, there would be
no number one.

Dad's dislike for certain books
is rule number two,
which stops me from reading
about a dinosaur that poo'd

The third rule requires me not
to scream or shout,
which is one of Dad's favourites,
of that there's no doubt.

Number four is something I find difficult to stop,
I keep asking for things when we go out to shop.

What can I say about rule number five,
It's to remember my manners, which is no surprise.

Next comes number six,
which is not even halfway,
I'm so tired of reading these,
and it's only midday.

I could tell that Dad wanted to make amends,
so we rush off to play, like the best of friends.

We run into the kitchen to create some slimy goo,
which makes funny noises, like you're going to the loo.

We play all over the house, from the living room to the garden,
Dad does smelly farts, loud burps and doesn't say pardon!

This is not the Dad I know, this boy's a bundle of fun.
He's just right for me, but he'll be too much for my mum.

Outside in the sunshine we go crazy on the swings,
then jump up and down, like our legs are made of springs.

Next we go on a treasure hunt to discover some hidden rubies, only for Dad to find them and pretend they're giant boobies.

At the end of the garden we climb up the old oak tree,
playing as we are, it's wonderful to feel so free.

Reaching the top, we enter a beautiful wooden home,
it's great to be with my dad, instead of being here alone.

Up in the tree house, he tells me he wants to be an explorer.
hacking through a jungle is very different to being a lawyer.

I'm having the best time, I don't want it to end,
but mum's getting suspicious about my new friend.

Laughing and playing, my dad's a real superstar,
the time we've had together has been the best by far.

We've been playing for hours, building up such a sweat,
but I need to turn him back, and do a Daddy reset.

With a wave of the crystal, he's back to how he used to be,
blissfully unaware of the fun we've had up a tree.

This power I have comes with great responsibility,
I love changing my dad from a bore into a liability.

The End, for now…